THE VESTIGES

THE VESTIGES

Jeff Derksen

TALONBOOKS

Talonbooks
P.O. Box 2076, Vancouver, British Columbia, Canada V6B 3S3
www.talonbooks.com

Typeset in Sabon
Printed and bound in Canada on 100% post-consumer recycled paper
Typeset and cover design by Typesmith
Cover and frontispiece: Alfredo Jaar, *Searching for Gramsci*, 2004

First printing: 2013

Talonbooks gratefully acknowledges the financial support of the Canada
Council for the Arts, the Government of Canada through the Canada Book
Fund, and the Province of British Columbia through the British Columbia
Arts Council and the Book Publishing Tax Credit.

The author is grateful to the Canada Council for the Arts for a grant that
assisted in the writing of this work.

Library and Archives Canada Cataloguing in Publication

Derksen, Jeff, 1958–, author
      The vestiges / Jeff Derksen.

Poems. ISBN 978-0-88922-794-1 (pbk.)

      I. Title.

PS8557.E5895V48 2013   C811'.54   C2013-903851-5

For Sabine

CONTENTS

The future will be visible
    to its particular philosophy
If so it will be
    teachable to photography

  – LYN HEJINIAN, *The Cell*

The true remake does not treat the past as a store of
models to be followed but as a smouldering problem:
the true remake is a haunted one.

  – SVEN LÜTTICKEN, "Planet of the Remakes"

The windmill itself they got from Germany, where its
invention called forth a petty squabble between the
nobility, the priests, and the Emperor as to which of
the three was the "owner" of the wind.

  – KARL MARX, *Capital,* Volume I

THE VESTIGES

1

Linear tankers lie
on the harbour's horizon.

The speed of globalization.

"Community-based
crystal-meth focus groups."
Jog by.

At sunset
crows crack mussels
at the empty pool, coast

above the transparent penthouse
a speculative building

on the edge
of the public park
capitalizing the view.

The silhouette swirls
her window cleaner
every Thursday. Realtors
facing west, make calls.

Lining up with the tide
China Shipping Line, the ships

rusted. Space
metabolized in the city

but secured
on the street
against riots

living through

"the shipwreck
of the singular."

Intensive ownership
spiralling up, making air
solid space
for the singular

as a structure
                    "is born and reborn
                    at the heart of
                    a contradiction"

of feeling

the building
is horrifying

in the materials

because it has no use.

"Who is not
for sustainability?"

outside
of such sincerity.

These machines
in the garden. "every day
more intense nature."
Post-punks in the park
against the state
or in nature.

Buildings as "machines
for living" even as
they are built
on a bubble.

"The machine is a means
for producing surplus value."

But not simply defined
by such surplus.

Blue plastic sheets strung up
in the tangle of trees
and stumps. A plywood platform.
For living, use.

The city scopes itself
through view corridors
that tunnel through
the common air

a commonwealth, a commodity.

"Any space that is organized around the monument is
colonized and oppressed."

What other present

seemed so endless, so
expendable.

Tell me what is necessary.

What is
necessary time.

What would we learn
by remaking the riots
with the roles reversed?

Coal miners' strike, nation pits
cops unions towns break down
"there is no such thing ..."
famously

[and fuck the Falklands.]
"I love a man

in a uniform." "The Call
Up." Our General
Strike called back

in the final moment, a historic
compromise.

"the shortest, surest and easiest
means of springing into
the better social future"
at one explosive point.

The retaking of the "heart
of the neighbourhood," the necessity
of a building autonomous
from a developer's city plan

then to see it given again.

The Gift Economy
after the shock of the private.

The Woodsquat
taught (history
teaches) the weak points
are lacunae to be taken.

A new global terrain.
Not sheep.

Hamburg, Park Fiction squat
looks down on
the new docks, a global waterfront
"kein Polizei kein Problem"
black letters on sheets waving from the windows.

Hotel Vancouver "invaded"
by returning soldiers 1946
without housing
and run it themselves.

The beloved boys
Regina 1935
"shot or sent back"
on the same trains
still without jobs.

Ottakring Februaraufstand 1934
"heavy fighting in the worker's housing"

but in another district
H. D. seemingly walks through
Vienna's barricades on her way
to see the Professor.

January 1958 Caracas
the superblocks, slabs
on the hills above the city
four thousand apartments

mass squatted
as Pérez Jiménez

flew to Miami
not out of
the goodness of his heart.

In 1905 one thousand slugs
of punctuation
"felling absolutism"
ended the aristocracy

as the word spread

as such.

Paving stones, and who's
on top, kicking off
an ultimate final offer

on the table, cutting the legs
out from under

and the fixed factory
itself cut up and shipped off.

We don't negotiate with
workers or terrorists post-Thatcher

Post-Mulroney
Post-Reagan
Post-Kohl
Post-NAFTA
Post–mega-event
Post–market bubble
Post-industrial
Post–port city
Post–big bailout
Post-G20
Post-drone

"a set of circumstances, a privileged
place" enclosed:

the names of those who walk
as heads of the town!

"Let them not talk of what is good for the city"

Local products that spread
as coercion | corruption | force.

Money changing hands – *like
it was material* –
in a brown paper bag

under the table of the convention centre
shaped like a ship
a decorated shed.

A new crass class
("wat about di workin' claas")
locked in competition

with each other!

The super-rich eat the rich
on a level playing field!

[East Van rules: the nŏun
the neon.]

"last of its kind"
or "only eleven left"
space scarcity

dwellings spilling off the hills
on the slopes to the sea's
abstract view. Abstract

paintings I walk by
downtown ("Downtown! Things
will be better when you're ...")

Cleaners also clean the lobbies
on temporary visas. Owned
by the owners.
Silhouetted. State

an outline
of a relationship.

"If the weak points
can thus be changed
into strong points ..."

As all the locksmiths of Sevilla
refuse to change
the locks
when the banks ask.

Look at the sun
sinking like a ship
into ships

their stacked coloured cube
containers abstracted

> "bygone instruments of labour"
> "extinct economic formation"
> "fossil bones."

What did the dinosaurs
invest in? What is the work week
of whales?

"From pins to people …"
it adds up.

Soft power over borders
holds or hoards bodies

when borders are hardened
today, the miracle
of social space
refracting "sheer life"

gold, growth industries
public-private partnerships

"bare / life"

that's legislation over flesh.

Isn't that the state
how it relates
to hollowed-out spaces?

Itself now hollow?

Nature
what have you done
for me
(that I could not do to you)?

"barbarism unifies nature"
that's an irony

to work against together.

Or how Shanghai is tied
to Prince George or what
Rotterdam could tell us.

Hamburg? Mumbai? Lagos?

as cities consolidate
into a texture.

Stadluft macht frei?
despite.

The crisis and then the
sell-off crisis and then the credit
crisis and then the confidence
crisis and then the jobs crisis.

Who knew? Capitalism
such a great surprise.

"Milton conveyed to millions
an understanding of the economic benefits
of free competitive markets ..."

to the bones (who
had them)

down to your bones.

How can one know.

2

Gas gouging? How
seventies!

Monopolies? How
Lenin!

Child labour? How
Dickens!

Bombing Baghdad
again? How nineties!

War crimes? How World
Court!

Apocalyptic
weather patterns? How
sci-fi!

Urban regeneration? How
organic!

Sustainable cities? How to
oust non-owners?

For the mayors of the
world, for the lords
of "zero tolerance," for the

presidents
of the building
for the captains
of commerce who

buy the names
of civic stadiums funded by
student bake sales.

The Utopie group
proposed a soft stadium
for five thousand in that "autumnal May."

Bolivians
stage a water strike instead.

Argentinians turn it
horizontal and

somewhere a pipeline
blows up in Canada.

Things with feelings
come and go
in a tanker over the ocean.

"Exception."

State. Awaits
a government
minister's antipathy.

We can't
be more specific than that.

"the task in Iraq"

carve up the remainder
of the world

before it turns
on you

you who have
extracted.

"Roger that."

Fifteen thousand feet
height of horizontal release.

3

The quiet diplomacy
of a world connected

by things used
every day and made
elsewhere. Easy.

This essay

sets out to explore
what happens

to humans when they are reduced
to things by other humans.

It's a novel about cities
in wartime

a poem about a people
in a distinct land, a time-based

performance piece about property
rights.

It's a short documentary
about walk-on construction
jobs.

But it's Monday, hours
harden into labour

shipped out of agreement zones
in the global south, daily
the stuff that

appears as a unity.

The texture of the everyday
of every city, the remaking
of its centre

constant creative destruction

on and off the waterfronts.

Is mixed use
sleeping in doorways

the grey economy
CDs cellphones tools cassettes batteries bikes lighters shoes
    watches clothes

spread on blankets
on the sidewalks

under the overhang
of a pawnshop awning

[consistently ranked number one
in the world].

Post-socialist Hungarian hills
and the verdant valleys

after the flood
of a deepened century.

Architecture
without architects

the railway workers' hut
between the tracks

graffiti thickening into
the central station.

Calgary suburban cul-de-sacs of social reproduction
circle the prairie with loops

dotted alongside the lines
of agribusiness.

Do you have to love
a city?

A hollow grain silo
on the flat lakefront
is a future tubular
condo in Toronto.

On the edge
of the East Bloc broken

housing blocks boarded and abandoned

pale-blue facades of the modular modernist
ambitions for a People

awaiting a use

that turns to speculation.

"Two types of freedom"
condensed to one.

Homes for America prefabbed
worldwide

strip shed duck ethnoburb exurb
a heroic singular process.

The song
of the shapes
from maps
seen from planes

the scales of place
used to "compel
the day"

(used to).

Abstracted as landscapes:

hard-edged industrialism
log booms on the rivers

piers sawtooth into inlets
detritus and works yards

casino zones, cars
the compact core
and the lights leading in

to the core.

"Once and for all that neither the slums
nor the tract houses

represent that apex
of the culture."

Permanent world

crisis balanced by cities

living through it.

[software update available]

4

"What they're going to say is:
lower the goals
forget about the democracy crap
put more resources in
do it":
unnamed official.

An economy of promises and gaps
made elsewhere

"It seems when Milton Friedman talked,
someone in Chile listened"

for
            the
                      taking.

"Who do you think
you are, you treacherous shits?"

[Marvin Gaye's "Let's Get It On"
was top of the charts
the day the tanks were in Santiago's streets.]

"¿Es usted feliz?"

The world makes
way for a third way

even after the primitive first.

"Preserving social protection
for the strong."

"In his career …
has so far not shown
any interest in poverty
reduction …"

as the World Bank head
explodes.

Let's get it on.

Primitive.

The economy is still screaming.

      "We had a small victory
          at city hall yesterday."

5

Bad history's black bridge
of the eighties

comes about through its opposite

a staging area, an ambassador
something not foreseen

to today
[name deleted:
Tegucigalpa inserted].

The Dirty Wars overturned time
and collapsed space!

And bodies.

The "stunningly simplified
strategic vision" exported
makes a geography

a pipeline as direct
as New Land Acts.

Sheep to wool to cotton to
bananas to coffee to oil to gold
to land, to space
even in the abstract
above and below.

If each coffee bean
is a failed form
of cosmopolitanism
from below

and commodities enter into us
as marvelous things, self-
fashioned

then I can never forget Ramón Lopez Salazar.

[Managua transforms
from "salsa city" to "mass
urban base"]

"It rained in the Brazilian coffee belt
over the weekend" and it rained

in our public places
across all indexes.

"Prices closed with declines."

Who wrote, as a remembrance:
Ramón Lopez Salazar
24/3/79
Patria
Libre
  o
Morir

Can you feel it ("feel it
all") more than Puerto Alegre.

October 1983, the New
Jewel Movement meets Clint Eastwood
in *Heartbreak Ridge*.

Grenada, the first country
I watched
get invaded onscreen.

On the eve of our General Strike
shaken out.

And today "polls indicating
that 63% of the public
supported the invasion"
of somewhere.

In the instrument
they have made.

Of "somewhere"!

"Nationalization has a long
and inglorious history of failure
around the world. We support
the Venezuelan people
and think this is an unhappy day
for them"
: spokesperson.

The new commons
and new enclosures

north > < south
< south north >
  Nosotros

So we try this together

6

Now that art
can be anything

a skull, a consortium

"the idea
of using our power
for moral good
in the world"

is set back
on the plaza

bronzed Seagram modernism

floating steel frame

clients, a technical lightness

of what was made
and what gave way

to new cascades
of fixed capital

"the wonder
of the arcades"

I'd love to live in
solid air

"is it any wonder"

Propelled by things
that bring us back
to ourselves
"human scale"

or something outside of ourselves.

Air and light
that made the solidity
of a building

and not its exchange
to a value
more than air

"a house of cards"
that houses rested on

derived

a short history
of the collapse
of space.
And again.

"¿Es usted feliz?"

Students in the streets.

Families in the abandoned
undead buildings. Neighbours
across the fence.

7

"all that is solid"
is solid again

gold, silver
nickel, copper, coal

"the power of the straight line"

mass-produced.

As for those who love
to be astonished

we
       don't
              do
                      body counts.

8

Mini tyranny!

From me to you

"Bring it on"

"It's always Tuesday."

9

A neighbourhood
on the verge

urban frontiers
named and renamed
new pioneers
on the skids

taste cultures

and neighbourhood shock therapy
right to the heart
heart of the city.

Rattling "Sunday morning
early dawning" and the alternative
economy

bottles and cans musical

in a cart
down the alley to the park.

Where things were once made
when an hour was material, at

hand, demands
for what you never had

"shiny shiny boots
of leather" lean against
a dumpster.

Hours add up to space
to live per square foot

"I am tired, I am weary"
worried to kiss the boot.

Youth of Eglington

Youth of el Vente Tres

Youth of South Surrey

Youth of Scarborough

Youth of Five Corners

Youth of La Paz

Youth of *les banlieues*

Youth of the plazas

Youth of the moment

10

"an object outside ourselves"

That petrol emotion
that market meltdown
that baton on bone.

"a thing"

What's gold doing
today?

What is copper
down to?

"I found a flaw

in the model

of how the world works."
(Greenspan)

Thought that cities
were the keg

that would reveal
what relations

what public histories
lay under
the paving stones

(which were arbitrary
for throwing).

"of what gets empowered
and
   what
      gets
         contained"

The city digs itself out
as others dig
themselves in

another
use for nature

music, acoustic

that late-sixties
ringing

"Where Evil Grows"

will it bring, will it
occupy
the libraries

the weak points then the strong points

an access
to a language

"only the image of a voice"

through a soft coup reduced to admiring his ruthlessness

so present
as to decompress

"shattered"
students shake blankets
from the library windows

taped up for the tear gas canisters
to come

"Spent a week in a dusty library
Waiting for some words to jump at me."

What we need
right now is

"fresh availability
of cheap labour"
and land

"and love sweet love."

Watching history:

"did not rise like the sun
at the appointed time. It was
present at its own making"

11

"At this point
I will no longer
refer to the city

                but

                    to

                         the

                              urban."

And the squander of people and place
"Tell me why"

"how I feel on the inside"
is not so different
from how it looks
on the outside.

      Embedded lyric fragment
      found where they still make
      ships, the port
      not split, but "opened
      to the sea"
      by the cruise ships' shopping space:

      I don't have a hard heart
      but capital has grizzled
      it up
      that and
      other crap
      crouched behind the monument
      to the fishing industry.

Expect
the exception today.

The one gives
way to
a way of life

less singular, less
solitary – the

horizontal lay of the body over the state.

That seems to be
the question today

if difference
is spreading

and often softer
words for privatization.

What augury or economy
has stuck it to
us so

"strategies for
outflanking
and the outflanking
of strategies."

The question
on the tip
of everyone's
device:

Service.
Open plan.
Leading to.

"Hundreds of black-hooded anarchists roamed the streets,
smashing store windows and hacking chunks of marble off
buildings to throw at police." [Greece]

"The rioting intensified into the night, with shop fronts
smashed and media vehicles damaged. Police charged
the crowds to seize individuals, and fired plastic bullets
in an effort to clear a park, Reuters news agency
reported." [Toronto]

Smuggled letter to Kevin and Dorothy

Now I fully understand your
"wholly owned subsidiary"
as a push back
against what felt like
in the descending time
after the General Strike's
deflection

really felt like
an attack
on life
as we were trying
to live it

at least east
of Main Street

where the wind
blew heavy along

the unemployment lines
and down to

the chicken-processing plant
off Cordova

we were working
hard to find a way of living

as the city faltered
and singular no more

keeping the "true
love of mine"

once was, a true
dividing line.

12

Another day
of managing
myself

Another day of
outflanking

Another day of
managing language
and management language

Another day of you and me
"under conditions
not of [our own] making"

Another day of
"markedly different"

Another day of street
in the city, promising

another day of the idea
of streets

Another day behind
the wheel
and of rubber hitting
the rub

another private day, another
making a day

Another day of
necessities

Another day of making
nature

Another day of
"Can the government actually do anything about
    inequality?"

Another day of
the movement of goods

Another day, another
attempt to prorogue

Another day
Another day upon arrival

13

The ships sit high
and empty. Spot-check price
on oil, pipelines stretching to
the northern port, spot-check
price on natural gas
let them sit high
against the incoming tide.

Each beaded seam
of those ships
was welded
somewhere, but not here.

Why lament capital
the vestiges of which
are not material, no wooden
brain could make me dance to that.

Why lament surplus
the vestiges of which
have become immaterial
even to its makers.

I want to shout out
to those whose lungs
died before they did
those whose lungs shared the air
of Machine Number 4
at Scott Paper, after
the pulp logs

came up from the Amazon
and those who flushed the effluent
at the river's high tide.

But is this lament
of labour a lament of
the vestiges of a form of labour
or a way seeing
labour, a way of seeing labour

just as it turned.

I lament that
surplus is violence.

A stark austerity is made
public, an urban life

a story made new again by its
circulation

the bombing of Guernica was ordered
from Lüneburg

the nightmare
(remember the eighties!)
of bodies absorbing the desires (code
word *liberation*) of capital
now is inverted

like the port
workers who moved
and made things

no more consumer citizen
in the *zócalo*
a national space, where, days before
the Olympics, on October 2
another example of force
over rights.

And is this not
expected today – tolerated
or truncheoned – "between equal
rights force decides"
the day, its length
and the idea of something
beyond that.

*Message mistakenly sent to Maximus and
undisclosed recipients*

I have had to learn
how to stop
being a prick.
It was tough, given
my training
It was tougher
given
the times.

Cars, finally
were not to be my trade
paper, instead
stepped in
patriarchally.

> We may all be belated
> and we are all
> uneven, multiple
> and multitude
> that's for mouths to chew
> that's for you.

I've sought what pleasures
paper and rubber
on the road
could give

but the world?
keeps on turning
more and more
and that is what you should
ask of me, more

and that is what
I should give

This difficult realm
of support for the port

workers, or "change the world
without taking power"

waterfronts invert themselves, turn
their own histories
it its head

to become themselves historical

as Monday morning opens
the city as if the city lives

zero degrees on the way
to work, and the idea of something

beyond that, to not
work, to not be worked

over as the simple
way to be in the world

the art of "not being governed
like that
and at that cost."

Some thing beyond a
subject, or a subject among
others, the simple
outcome of democracy's deficit

its restraints felt
in the austere choice

of politics or post-politics
where we are then tempted

with a community to come
in the place

of "overturn" and "total life"

14

Bourdieu: "Paris, December 1995

The railway workers, postal workers, teachers, civil servants, students and many others, actively or passively engaged in the movement, have, through their demonstrations and declarations, through the countless rethinkings that they have provoked, which the media cannot put the lid on, raised quite fundamental problems ... What I wanted to express, in any case, perhaps clumsily – and I apologize to those who I may have shocked or bored – is a real solidarity with those who are now fighting to change

society."

"I WELCOME EVERY OPINION BASED ON SCIENTIFIC CRITICISM" (or, all of the sentences containing the first-person pronoun in Marx's *Capital*, Volume 1, excluding the prefaces, the footnotes, and sentences quoted from other authors, but including the characterizations of the capitalist and the worker)

I was the first to point out and examine critically this twofold nature of the labour contained in commodities.

I refer to the money-form.

I cannot, for example, express the value of linen in linen.

But in this case I must reverse the equation, in order to express the value of the coat relatively; and, if I do that, the linen becomes the equivalent instead of the coat.

I mean Aristotle.

I call this the fetishism which attaches itself to the products of labour as soon as they are produced as commodities, and is therefore inseparable from the production of commodities.

If I state that coats or boots stand in relation to linen because the latter is the universal incarnation of abstract human labour, the absurdity of the statement is self-evident.

Throughout this work I assume that gold is the money commodity, for the sake of simplicity.

I know nothing of a man if I merely know his
name is Jacob.

The leap taken by value from the body of the commodity
into the body of the gold is the commodity's *salto mortale*,
as I have called it elsewhere.

If I purchase 2,000 lb. of cotton for £100, and resell the
2,000 lb. of cotton for £110, I have in fact exchanged £100
for £110, money for money.

If I sell a quarter of corn for £3, and with this £3 buy clothes,
the money so far as I am concerned, is irreversibly spent.

I have nothing more to do with it.

If I now sell a second quarter of corn, money indeed flows
back to me, not however as a result of the first transaction,
but of its repetition.

The money again leaves me as soon as I complete this
second transaction by a fresh purchase.

As a capitalist, I buy commodities from A and sell them
again to B, but as a simple owner of commodities I sell
them to B and then purchase further commodities from A.

I myself confront them each time as a mere owner of either
money or commodities, as a buyer or a seller, and what is
more, in both sets of transactions I confront A only as a
buyer and B only as a seller.

I confront the one only as money, the other only as commodities, but neither or [sic] them as capital or a capitalist, or a representative of anything more than money or commodities, or of anything which might produce any effect beyond that produced by money or commodities.

And if I offered to explain to them the meritorious nature of my action in inverting the order of succession, they would probably point out to me that I was mistaken as to that order, and that the whole transaction, instead of beginning with a purchase and ending with a sale, began, on the contrary, with a sale and was concluded with a purchase.

"I might have squandered the 15 shillings, but instead I consumed it productively and made yarn with it."

"Did I not provide him with the materials through which, and in which alone, his labour could be embodied?"

"And as the greater part of society consists of such impecunious creatures, have I not rendered society an incalculable service by providing my instruments of production, my cotton and my spindle, and the worker too, for have I not provided him with the means of subsistence?"

"Am I to be allowed nothing in return for all this service?"

Our friend, who has up till now displayed all the arrogance of capital, suddenly takes on the assuming demeanour of one of his own workers, and exclaims: "Have I myself not worked? Have I not performed the labour of superintendence, of overseeing the spinner?"

For this reason, I call it the constant part of capital, or more briefly, constant capital.

I therefore call it the variable part of capital, or more briefly, variable capital.

I call the portion of the working day during which this reproduction takes place necessary labour-time, and the labour expended during that time necessary labour; necessary for the worker, because independent of the particular social form of his labour; necessary for capital and the capitalist world, because the continued existence of the worker is the basis of that world.

This part of the working day I call surplus labour-time, and to the labour expended during that time I give the name of surplus labour.

Suddenly, however, there arises the voice of the worker, which had previously been stifled in the sound and fury of the production process: "The commodity I have sold you differs from the ordinary crowd of commodities in that its use creates value, a greater value than it costs."

"You and I know on the market only one law, that of the exchange of commodities."

"But by means of the price you pay for it every day, I must be able to reproduce it every day, thus allowing myself to sell it again."

"Apart from natural deterioration through age etc., I must be able to work tomorrow with the same normal amount of strength, health and freshness as today."

"Like a sensible, thrifty owner of property I will husband my sole wealth, my labour-power, and abstain from wasting it foolishly."

"Every day I will spend, set in motion, transfer into labour only as much of it as is compatible with its normal duration and healthy development."

"By an unlimited extension of the working day, you may in one day use up a quantity of labour-power greater than I can restore in three."

"What you gain in labour, I lose in the substance of labour."

"I therefore demand a working day of normal length, and I demand it without any appeal to your heart, for in money matters sentiment is out of place."

"I demand a normal working day because, like every other seller, I demand the value of my commodity."

I can therefore express the same relation by saying for instance that in every minute the worker works 30 seconds for himself and 30 seconds for the capitalist, etc.

I call that surplus-value which is produced by the lengthening of the working day, *absolute surplus-value.*

In contrast to this, I call that surplus-value which arises from the curtailment of the necessary labour-time, and from the corresponding alteration in the respective lengths of the two components of the working day, *relative surplus-value*.

On the other hand, as I have already remarked, the exchange of products springs up at the points where different families, tribes or communities come into contact; for at the dawn of civilization it is not private individuals but families, tribes, etc. that meet on an independent footing.

The rules of the guilds, as I have said before, deliberately hindered the transformation of the single master into a capitalist, by placing very strict limits on the number of apprentices he could employ.

Modern manufacture – I am not referring here to large-scale industry, which is based on machinery – either finds the *disjecta membra poetae* ready to hand, and only waiting to be collected together, as is the case in the manufacture of clothes in large towns, or it can easily apply the principles of division, simply by exclusively assigning the various operations of a handicraft (such as book-binding) to particular men.

I come back to this example in order to clear up an erroneous notion.

I shall pass over the experiments made in the spinning and carding rooms, because they were accompanied by an increase of 2 per cent in the speed of the machines.

For the present I will say only this: workers who have been thrown out of work in a given branch of industry can no doubt look for employment in another branch.

In the few remarks I have still to make on this point, I shall refer in part to relations of a purely practical nature, the existence of which has not yet been revealed by our theoretical presentation.

I give on the opposite page a summary of the result.

I shall now illustrate the principles laid down above with a few examples.

There is a rich collection of official material to be found in the fourth and sixth *Public Health Reports* (1862 and 1864) on the way in which capital economizes on the requirements for labour in modern manufacture (in which I include all workshops on a large scale, except factories proper).

I now come to so-called domestic industry.

For the sake of conciseness, I have classified them under headings.

I should also add that every question and its obligatory answer are numbered in the English Blue Books, and that the witnesses whose depositions are cited here are all workers in coal mines.

However, all I wish to point out here is that there exists an irresistible tendency towards the general application of those principles.

I assume (1) that commodities are sold at their value, (2) that the price of labour-power occasionally rises above its value, but never sinks below it.

I shall show in Volume 3 that the same rate of surplus-value may be expressed in the most diverse rates of profit, and that different rates of surplus-value may, under certain circumstances, be expressed in the same rate of profit.

There is a third formula, which I have occasionally anticipated:

$$\frac{\text{Surplus-value}}{\text{Value of labour-power}} = \frac{\text{Surplus labour}}{\text{Necessary labour}} = \frac{\text{Unpaid labour}}{\text{Paid labour}}$$

I give, in conclusion, a comparative table of Mr. Redgrave's on the average number of spindles per factory and per spinner in the different countries of Europe.

In the third part of Volume 2 I shall give an analysis of the way the whole system is actually linked together.

I call the former the value-composition, the latter the technical composition of capital.

To express this, I call the value-composition of capital, in so far as it is determined by its technical composition and mirrors the changes in the latter, the organic composition of capital.

Wherever I refer to the composition of capital, without further qualification, its organic composition is always understood.

I shall come back to the agricultural labourers later on.

On the condition of urban dwellings, I quote, as a preliminary, a general remark made by Dr. Simon.

I shall merely glance at their housing conditions.

Before I turn to the agricultural labourers, I shall just show, by one example, how crises have an impact even on the best paid section of the working class, on its aristocracy.

Before I turn to his present situation, a rapid look back.

From the tables appended to the first volume of the Report I have compiled this comparative summary.

I give below a short selection of examples, gathered from a dozen counties.

The finest fruit of this vicious circle thrives in the east of England – this is the so-called gang-system, to which I must briefly return here.

(he means his "hands"
who work for "us")

(Does this Mr. Smith take no meals
himself during 10½ hours?)

(this same Smith)
(he means leave off
from consuming "our" labour-power machines)
(the same man again)
(152 children and young persons
and 140 adults)
(1862)
(a district of London)
(!)
(What generosity!)
(as we see from the poets of the Roman Empire)
(We shall disregard the practice
of making bread
by machinery, which has only recently begun to make
its way here.)
1855–6)
at the close of the Parliamentary Session of 1863)
sometimes very short)
who sell their bread under
the full price, and who, as already
pointed out, comprise three-fourths
of the London bakers)

All this refers to
Sunday labour)

The smaller and the medium farmers – I reckon among these all who do not cultivate more than 100 acres – still make up about 8/10 of the whole number.

From the mass of material that lies before me, I give a few extracts chosen for the strong light they throw on the circumstances of the time.

Where these labour-statutes aim at a compulsory extension of the working day, I shall not return to them, as we discussed this point earlier (in Chapter 10, Section 5).

THE PARENTHETICAL

Silvia Federici
"Wages against Housework," *Revolution at Point Zero*

(The magic words:
"Yes, darling, you are a real woman")

(which are relations of loneliness)
(but to work in a factory is already a defeat)

(Until recently airline stewardesses in the United States
were periodically weighed

and had to be constantly on a diet
– a torture that all women know –

for fear of being laid off)
(by ourselves, in groups)

(i.e., to serve them)
(capital has disciplined them through us

and us through them –
each other, against each other)

(productivity)
(female productivity)

Karl Marx
"The Working Day," *Capital*, **Volume 1**

(while doing a reasonable amount of work)

(1867)

(sometimes more, sometimes less)
(sometimes more, sometimes less)
(sometimes more, sometimes less)

(allowing two for holidays
and occasional stoppages)

(cleaning their machinery, etc.)

(over-looking the violation of the Act)

(as I was informed
by a highly respectable master)

(carried ready-moulded articles into the dryin
afterwards bringing back the empty mould)

(for dinner)
(1863)

(block printing)
(evening)

(in that land of Sabbatarians!)

(in some cases from 6)
(i.e. the subject of restrictions on night-work)
(Messrs Naylor & Vickers, on the other
hand, in line with the best interests
of their business, took the opposite view, that periodic
alterations of night and day-labour
well do more harm
than continual night-labour.)

(What cynical naïveté!)
(What mealy-mouthed phraseology!)

(In other words, Ellis, or Brown & Co.
might be subjected
to the fatal embarrassment
of having to pay
labour-power at its full value.)
(how wrong-headed these
people are!)
("generally," but of course,
not always "in particular")
(instead of the present waste
of the living substance
of the workers)

(whereas a loss of sleeping time,
even that of 8-year-olds, is a gain
of working time for the Sanderson clan)

(whereas those same furnaces
suffer nothing
from the alteration of day-work
and night-work)

(and that in a country of Sabbatarians!)

(Mr. Villiers, President of
The Poor Law Board)

(profit)
(23 Edward III, 1349)

(not its cause, for legislation
of this kind outlives its pretext by centuries)
(i.e. at a price that left
their employers a reasonable quantity
of surplus labour)
(Henry VII)
("artificers")

(the meaning then
was "agricultural labourers")
(The agricultural labourers, however,
formed an exception.)

(he means capital, as we
shall soon see)
(the worker)

[i.e. the manufacturing worker]
[i.e. the agricultural labourers]

(in one word, paupers)

(i.e. persons between 13 and 18 years of age)
("relay" means, in English also in French, the
changing of post-horses at each
different halting-place)
(the factory method)
(which also administered freedom
drop by drop)
(1844)
(i.e. at meal times)
(from 13 to 18)
(in consequence of
the terrible crisis of 1846–7)

(so many spinners
getting very low wages
by having to work as piecers,
being unable to do better)

(for meals)

(1 hour)
(2 hours)
(3 ½ hours)

(Lancashire)
(1863)
(not just the potteries)

(from 8 in the evening
to 6 in the morning)

(the beginning of September 1866)

Silvia Federici
"Why Sexuality Is Work," *Revolution at Point Zero*

(we will have coffee together
as we get ready for work)

(finally)
(and thereby become clean)
(something that is not expected of most jobs)

(in marriage
or out of the home)

BUT WHAT OF THE CITY ITSELF?

For Neil Smith

In Buenos Aires in 1985, it was no longer possible to buy anything at night for what it had cost in the morning.

So what, exactly, happened in 1848 in Paris?

Visiting Las Vegas in the mid-1960s was like visiting Rome in the late 1940s.

By the middle of the 1990s, large chunks of Toronto sat expectantly waiting to be developed, reused, and recycled in the boom that had started in the real estate industry.

Before the fiscal crisis of the mid-1970s, New York was possibly the most egalitarian of any American city.

In June 1956, the city of Poznan witnessed Poland's first use of the mass inter-enterprise strike combined with street demonstrations.

I had not planned on coming back to Vienna, but a lot had happened between the summer of 1933 and the autumn of 1934.

The Woodwards building was opened on Saturday, September 14th, for free housing by a small group of housing activists and squatters from all around Vancouver.

Florence, a free city, contracted to surrender its freedom a second time, in 1322, to the King of Naples, in return for his protection.

Chicago's antislavery forces had tried to elect a mayor in 1841 and failed.

The closest it came was with the Tripoli Program, written in May 1962 for the party's congress in the Libyan capital.

And in the streams near the city, fishing was diligently pursued: Augsburg, for example, was noted for its trout, and until 1643 many of the city officials took their pay in trout.

Birmingham had four thousand at the first date and almost thirty thousand in 1760.

Likewise, as the rich began to abandon the center of Montevideo in the 1970s and 1980s for the attractive neighborhood of the east coast, homeless people moved into abandoned houses and derelict hotels.

Again the St. Petersburg general strike of 1896 appears as a purely economic partial wage struggle.

Domesticated plants appear in Sumer about 5000 B.C., while Eridu – the first city that we know of in that area – existed by 4000 B.C., housing several thousand persons.

Since the mid-1980s, the great industrial cities in the south – Bombay, Johannesburg, Buenos Aires, Belo Horizonte, and

São Paulo – have all suffered massive plant closures and tendential deindustrialization.

Toronto's first happening is said to have taken place in 1959 in the studio of Dennis Burton, whose fellow participants were Gordon Rayner, Graham Coughtry and CBC writer Murray Jessel.

Up until the early 1960s, Montreal still seemed to be what it had been: an English city with many French-speaking workers and inhabitants.

They demanded that New York Museums be shut down on May 22, seeking to stop business as usual for one day as a gesture of protest against U.S. military involvement in Vietnam.

In the middle of December in the year 1951, a locale opened in the heart of Vienna called the Strohkoffer [Straw Suitcase], taking its name from the reeds that lined its walls.

On the morning of June 20, the art gallery was emptied by the Vancouver Police, using tear gas.

Work began in 1951 on a series of gigantic housing schemes on the hills around Caracas with the intention of eradicating all slums – not out of the goodness of Pérez Jiménez's heart, but because they were unsightly and gave the lie to the slogan that Venezuela was uniformly happy and prosperous.

The proletariat of Paris was robbed by Bonaparte of its leaders, the barricade commanders, in a sudden attack on the night of 1–2 December.

In response to this, garden advocates organized a "roving garden party" to call attention to New York's fifty endangered community gardens in June 2007.

Between 1951 and 1956 Syracuse lost nearly 3000 elms.

The last to burn down in Chicago was the J.R Plaza Hotel, more commonly known as the Zanzibar, on February 14, 1999.

Thus the main Berlin Olympic Stadium, an emblem in 1936 for the Nazi Olympics, has now lost those associations in the eyes of those who visit it regularly to watch football matches.

During the latter part of the 1960s and into the 1970s, New York became increasingly beset by conflict between urban bureaucracies, still strongly white dominated, and their black and Hispanic clients.

In 2003 the fourteen housing associations of Amsterdam owned 55 percent of the total stock.

In the late 1970s, Ceausescu began his project of rebuilding the centre of Bucharest so that the architectural reality would properly reflect the greatness of Romanian communism.

In the meantime, there were to be isolated and expensive installations in luxury homes, some, indeed before 1930, such as those in the Chicago area by the redoubtable Samuel R. Lewis.

The most spectacular action by the Young Workers was the storming of Milan's La Scala in December 1976, which ended with several thousand proletarian youth looting luxury shops in the city center.

In the late 1960s, the leading banks of Frankfurt began an ambitious restructuring of the city into a bank and service industry metropolis.

He is speaking of Manchester in 1862.

Because of Picasso's artistry, it is widely believed that the first aerial bombing of a concentrated civilian target was the Luftwaffe's raid against Guernica, Spain, in 1934.

In 1895, the liberal bastion, Vienna, was engulfed in a Christian Social tidal wave.

By 432 Athens was so overbuilt indeed that refugees were forced to encamp on the Acropolis, in defiance of sound warnings against this foul concentration issued from Delphi itself.

Indeed, an incredible 85 percent of Kenya's population growth between 1989 and 1999 was absorbed in the fetid, densely packed slums of Nairobi and Mombasa.

In October of 1969, for instance, the N.E. Thing Co. invited students to come up with an artistic response to instructions sent from Vancouver.

But unlike San Diego in 1912, order in public discourse is not defined solely by the exclusion of disorder.

In fact, the massive destruction of old buildings and lifestyles impaired Beijing's attempt to apply for world heritage listing in 2000 and 2001.

In Turin in March 1973 a group of mainly young, autonomously organized workers, some armed and masked with red bandanas, occupied Mirafiori and other Fiat factories for several days following the failure of an all-out strike, violently rejecting any kind of union-management negotiation.

Such benevolence toward homeless people in Seattle had its limits, even in the 1980s.

The largest population of pavement dwellers in the Third World is probably in Mumbai, where 1995 research estimated one million living on the sidewalks.

The Catalans became great salt cod enthusiasts and brought it to southern Italy when they took control of Naples in 1443.

On the morning of 5 May, the mayor of Chicago declared a "state of war" in the city.

Class antagonism that had smoldered under the authoritarian social measures of the Second Empire intensified: on March 18, 1871, workers, many of them women who had borne the brunt of the hardships of the long Prussian siege of Paris, revolted.

How could Lagos in the 1980s grow twice as fast as the Nigerian population, while its urban economy was in deep recession?

It was during this period, from 1970 to 1974, that the Frankfurt squatters movement developed.

Despite the speed with which U.S. forces took Baghdad in 2003, urban war has probably changed less than most other forms of war.

Even in Beijing in 1985 only 1,107 cars were owned by households in Beijing; most people travelled on bicycles and buses.

Montreal's Victoria Day celebrations in May of 1963 were dreaded more than usual.

The reaction of the Green party to the Kreuzberg riot of May 1, 1987, was similar.

By the later 1960s Brasilia was the seat of a vicious military dictatorship ruling over economic crisis – by which time, to paraphrase Serge Guilbault, the USA had stolen the idea of modern architecture.

His example of how "iron, concrete, and cement are insulted" was Moscow's historicist Kazan Railway Station and its architect Shchusev (although his name is not mentioned), who won the job in 1911 and was still completing it.

Having rehoused the homeless and abolished most urban shantytowns by 1960, Beijing continued to exercise extraordinary vigilance over informal rural immigration.

On 6 December 2008, fifteen-year-old Alexis was shot by the police on an Athenian square, an event that triggered weeks of violent urban protests and that cascaded throughout Greece.

Indeed, if Cor van Eesteren's Amsterdam be excepted, between 1930 and 1940 the ideal of the European Constructivist movements, the ideal that had given life to a city of one unified tendency, was decidedly in crisis.

In the specific field of architecture, the crisis exploded in 1930 in Berlin Siemensstadt.

This has been the case in São Paulo, where Workers' Party (PT) administrations, starting in 1989, have tried to regularize and upgrade the "huge illegal city" of the poor.

In 1387 there were 29 bathmen in Frankfurt; in 1530, none.

Saskatoon's early settlers were too flushed with boomtown success to consider orderly growth as their community sprang from a frontier village of 113 people to a flourishing city of 21,000 by 1916.

On May 30, 1520, a crowd of woolworkers seized a hated member of Segovia's *Cortes* delegation and hanged him, leading to a revolt in the city that forced all its royal officials to take to their heels.

The same situation occurred in Newark (New Jersey) in 1967 and 1968, when the black community opposed the introduction of a medical school in the city center that involved the displacement of residents.

Meanwhile Los Angeles's deadline for compliance with the 1970 federal Clean Air Act expired.

On 18 November 1970, a demonstration, involving several thousand people and supported by several left-wing organizations, paralysed the center of Paris and revealed the emergence of a new protest movement on a question that had long been felt as something one could do nothing about.

That is Rietveld's use of a lowered, luminous ceiling in the corner house of a terrace in Utrecht built in 1930–1931.

The building was bombed by NATO in 1999, sold in 2002, and transformed into a business centre and symbol for the rapidly spreading new ideology in New Belgrade.

In 1843, among the accidents brought to the Infirmary in Manchester, one hundred and eighty-nine were from burning.

But in New York City, the size of the industrial workforce peaked in 1947.

On February 12th of that year the tallest tree on the Vancouver townsite was felled.

Indeed, when Malcolm X was assassinated in 1968, Toronto's Native activists co-sponsored a memorial for the martyred black leader with their African Canadian counterparts.

Phoenix was slow to accept federal funding for urban renewal projects in the 1960s.

Wagner soon found himself plunged into the great engineering project related to it: the construction of the Vienna city railway system in 1894–1901.

By the end of May 1974, workers' commissions, councils, and committees had been formed at almost all workplaces in the Lisbon region.

Try to imagine the lives these militants lived in the Chicago of the 1880s, among the slaughterhouses and smokestacks, in this babel of a thousand tongues and nationalities, the stink of butcher meat and train smoke heavy in the air.

And in 1910, the tertiary industry that sets Los Angeles apart even from other cities that now possess the same tertiary, was founded, when the first Hollywood movie was made in a barn at the corner of Sunset and Gower.

In the 1960s and 1970s, some new industrial satellite towns were built around cities like Beijing and placed downwind of the city.

London, like New York, had seen its commercial property crash during the mid-1970s as a consequence of rising interest rates and slackened demand.

The English Peasant Rebellion of 1381, which followed the French *Jacquerie* by less than three decades, formed a high point in the restive village upsurges that finally led to the brief seizure of London by a peasant army.

In Hamburg's Schanzenviertel, the conflict came to a head in 1988, when various groups protested the old theater house Flora being turned into a commercial cultural center.

In Riga, Latvia, and Reykjavík, Iceland, in early 2009, violent demonstrations led to the fall of elected governments.

On July 1, 1917, the Society's new board declared to its members: "Before us stands a ruined Moscow, a new social environment and entirely new legal norms, under which the work of architects must proceed in quite new directions."

At the end of a July 1 march against police brutality in Barcelona, a Milanese activist from the Tute Bianche took the microphone and announced the coming siege of the G8 summit.

The first of these bloody riots in the northern industrial cities occurred in 1917, in East St. Louis.

Yet, Mumbai after 9/11 had its own ways of registering the anxiety about Pakistan and the nervousness about its own large Muslim populations.

In 1999, New York City announced the imminent closure of its only landfill, Fresh Kills, the largest dump in the world.

At 4 a.m. on the morning of 5 January, while Montreal was asleep, a radio announcer warned that a powerful low-pressure system bearing down on Quebec from the Gulf of St. Lawrence might bring freezing rain and ice.

In early February 1974, another important Frankfurt squat, "The Block," was evicted in a surprise attack of 2,500 police.

The earlier rise of a significant youth movement (given to political satire) and the arrival of a freewheeling pop culture in the "swinging London" of the 1960s both mocked and challenged the traditional structure of networked class relations.

The occupation began on Tuesday, February 3, when about two dozen phone workers in Nanaimo and Duncan on Vancouver Island were suspended for "going slow."

In 1880, the first anti-Semitic Society for the Defense of the Handworker was founded in Vienna.

All the more so because New York's reign, like Paris's when Benjamin came to construct his elaborate intellectual billet-doux during the 1930s, is now over.

During the month that preceded the September 1970 elections, tens of thousands of people occupied sites in Santiago.

Despite these indicators of normalcy, the abrupt collapse of the region's economy after 2007 showed how much of Phoenix's buoyancy relied on the single factor of servicing population growth.

Of special significance were the closures of the Duffey Lake Road in the summer of 1990 (which cut off the towns of Pemberton from the east and Lillooet from the west) and the Stó:lö blockade on the main CN Rail line into Vancouver in 1993 (which cost CN around $3 million a day).

Here color coded characters from the celebrated revolutionary assignation of Gracchus Babeuf reappear on the streets of Paris in 1975; the citizenry, equally anonymous, embodies the critical mass of the people.

In September 2007 and February 2008 the Mahalla workers struck again, pushing the whole Egyptian working class forward.

The night of September 16, 1976, has remained in sad remembrance in La Plata as the "Night of the Pencils."

Overall, the thirty-five years from 1975 to 2010 marked the transformation of New York into a global city characterized by greater inequality and diminished democracy.

Democratic institutions persisted in a truncated form long after Athens's final defeat by the Macedonians at Krannon in 322 B.C.

It is never too late to revert to the subject of Herbert Marcuse and his brief stay in Paris in May 1968.

In February 1998, Grupo de Arte Callejero began setting up denunciatory signs in Buenos Aires.

Likewise, after the first Zeppelin attack on London in the spring of 1915, the city's concerned bird lovers, led by W.H. Hudson, author of the magisterial 1895 *Birds in London* (and, as we saw earlier, *A Crystal Age*) deployed to see if the bombing was scaring away birds from the city.

On Friday, 29 September 1843, an attempt was made to blow up the saw-works of Padgin, in Howard Street, Sheffield.

Dublin, in fact, suffered more from the problems of de-industrialization than from industrialization between 1800 and 1850.

This is what happened in the case of the Los Angeles riots of April 1992, attributed solely to the fact that several white policemen had been absolved of savagely beating a Black man.

The 18 days of protest on the now world famous Tahrir
Square in Cairo, Egypt, has come to symbolize the Arab
uprisings of 2011.

Until 1838 neither Manchester nor Birmingham even
functioned politically as incorporated boroughs: they
were man-heaps, machine warrens, not agents of human
association for the promotion of a better life.

Between the 1900s and the 1930s, during the height of
Paris's reign as art capital of the world, there was a boom in
building of studio-houses.

The art and literature that's being made in Vancouver now
is not necessarily that much better than what was being
made here in 1958.

Yet even these authors do not mention the flushing W.C.,
for instance, without which such tower blocks would
be uninhabitable, nor the various devices required to
combat the thermal and ventilating peculiarities of the
skyscraper as it had become established In Chicago and
New York by 1900.

The last three miles of the river form a sheltered deepwater
harbor, and in 1207, King John granted permission for a
town to be built there, which was called Liverpool.

In the center of the city, along the banks of the
Chicago River, a small community of the free had been
growing since 1840.

THE PARENTHETICAL

Louis Althusser
"Ideological State Apparatus (Notes towards an Investigation),"
Lenin and Philosophy and Other Essays

(reproducing exactly the previous conditions of production)

(expanding them)

(since *Capital* Volume Two)

(ideological obviousnesses of an empiricist type)

(itself abstract in relation to the process of production)

(worse than one-sided: distorted)

(including the bourgeois economists whose work is national accounting, or the modern "macro-economic" "theoreticians")

(buildings)

(machines)

(for reproduction)

(production of means of production)

(production of means of consumption)

(the wherewithal to pay for housing, food and clothing, in short to enable the wage earner to present himself again at the factory gate the next day – and every further day God grants him)

(in n models where $n = 0, 1, 2$, etc ...)

(wages)

(*Salaire Minimum Interprofessionnel Garanti*)

(Marx noted that English workers need beer while French proletarians need wine)

(a double class struggle: against the lengthening of the working day and against the reduction of wages)

(diversely)

(diversified)

(this is a tendential law)

(apprenticeship within production itself)

(which may be rudimentary or on the contrary thoroughgoing)

(one instruction for manual workers, another for technicians, a third for engineers, a final one for higher management, etc.)

(for the future capitalists and their servants)

(ideally)

(but also other State institutions like the Church, or other apparatuses like the Army)

(Marx)

(the proletarians)

(the capitalists)

(the managers)

(its "functionaries")

(and this thesis only repeats famous propositions of historical materialism)

(the "unity" of the productive forces and the relations of production)

(law and the State)

(the different ideologies, religious, ethical, legal, political, etc.)

(it reveals the difference between Marx and Hegel)

(infrastructure)

(*topique*)

(in the air)

(of the superstructure)

(as yet undefined)

(or determination)

(1)

(2)

(base and superstructure)

(or of index of effectivity)

(and therefore to answer them)

(and in all the later classical texts, above all in Marx's writings on the Paris Commune and Lenin's on *State and Revolution*)

(in the nineteenth century the bourgeois class and the "class" of big landowners)

(i.e. to capitalist exploitation)

(in the narrow sense)

(the proletariat has paid for this experience with its blood)

(infrastructure and superstructure)

(descriptive)

(that of the science of social formations)

(1)

(2)

(and relatively anodyne)

(imperialist wars)

(and its existence in its apparatus)

(conservation of State power or seizure of State power)

(1830, 1848)

(2 December, May 1958)

(the fall of the Empire in 1870, of the Third Republic in 1940)

(1890–95 in France)

(1)

(2)

(3)

(or alliance of classes or of fractions of classes)

(4)

(the end of State power, the end of every State apparatus)

(repressive)

(ISAs)

(repressive)

(SA)

(since repression, e.g. administrative repression, may take non-physical forms)

(the order in which I have listed them has no particular significance)

(the system of the different Churches)

(the system of the different public and private "Schools")

(the political system, including the different Parties)

(press, radio and television, etc.)

(Literature, the Arts, sports, etc.).

(Repressive)

(Repressive)

(Repressive)

(in their apparent dispersion)

(subordinate)

(Repressive)

(Repressive)

(Repressive)

(including physical repression)

(There is no such thing as a purely repressive apparatus.)

(There is no such thing as a purely ideological apparatus.)

(censorship, among other things)

(predominantly, secondarily)

(Repressive)

(Repressive)

(openly or more often by means of alliances between classes or class fractions)

(Repressive)

(Repressive)

(among others)

(or class alliance)

(repressive)

(and its possession by ...)

(Infrastructure, Superstructure)

(Repressive)

(Repressive)

(Repressive)

(Repressive)

(physical or otherwise)

(the capitalist State contains political dynasties, military dynasties, etc.)

(from the most brutal physical force, via mere administrative commands and interdictions, to open and tacit censorship)

(sometimes teeth-gritting)

(usually called the feudal mode of production)

(the religious Ideological State Apparatus)

(the Estates General, the *Parlement*, the different political factions and Leagues, the ancestors of the modern political parties, and the whole political system of the free Communes and then of the *Villes*)

(the powerful merchants' and bankers' guilds and the journeymen's associations, etc.)

(e.g., the national popular Army)

(Louis XVIII and Charles X)

(Louis-Philippe)

(de Gaulle)

(peace among all men of good will in the ruling classes!)

(epitomized by Bismarck)

(parliamentary)

(plebiscitary or fascist)

(the role of sport in chauvinism is of the first importance)

(those of the remnants of former ruling classes, those of the proletarians and their organizations)

(French, arithmetic, natural history, the sciences, literature)

(ethics, civic instruction, philosophy)

(capitalists, managers)

(soldiers, policemen, politicians, administrators, etc.)

(priests of all sorts, most of whom are convinced "laymen")

(with a "highly developed" "professional," "ethical," "civic," "national" and a-political consciousness)

(ability to give the workers orders and speak to them: "human relations")

(ability to give orders and enforce obedience "without discussion," or ability to manipulate the demagogy of a political leader's rhetoric)

(ability to treat consciousnesses with the respect, i.e. with the contempt, blackmail, and demagogy they deserve, adapted to the accents of Morality, of Virtue, of "Transcendence," of the Nation, of France's World Role, etc.)

(modesty, resignation, submissiveness on the one hand, cynicism, contempt, arrogance, confidence, self-importance, even smooth talk and cunning on the other)

(and not least, free)

(because it is ... lay)

(in complete confidence)

(who are free, too, i.e. the owners of their children)

(the majority)

(which is bigger than they are and crushes them)

(the famous new methods!)

(already proclaimed in the *Communist Manifesto*)

(and the School-Family couple)

(genetic)

(we shall see why in a moment)

(most visibly, the ideology of the vulgar economists)

(religious, ethical, legal, political)

(defined in the double respect suggested above: regional and class)

(meaning also the other forms of ideology)

(*bricolé*)

(since in this book philosophy is ideology *par excellence*)

(*bricolage*)

(manufactured by who knows what power: if not by the

alienation of the division of labour, but that, too, is a
negative determination)

(on the contrary, for it is merely the pale, empty and inverted
reflection of real history)

("ideology has no history")

(although it is determined in the last instance by the
class struggle)

(its history is external to it)

(and in a way which has absolutely nothing arbitrary about
it, but, quite the reverse, is theoretically necessary, for there
is an organic link between the two propositions)

(temporal)

(= the history of social formations containing social classes)

(e.g., "believe" in God, Duty, Justice, etc ...)

(ideology = *illusion/allusion*)

(God is the imaginary representation of the real King)

(to Feuerbach, for example, God is the essence of real Man)

(and inversion)

(that of the eighteenth century)

(that of Feuerbach, taken over word for word by Marx in his Early Works)

(= imaginary)

(in the *1844 Manuscripts*: because these conditions are dominated by the essence of alienated society – "*alienated labour*")

(if we do not live in its truth)

(and the other relations that derive from them)

(imaginary)

(individual)

(Priests or Despots)

(*idéale* or *idéelle*)

(*idéale, idéelle*)

(the unity of these different regional ideologies – religious, ethical, legal, political, aesthetic, etc. – being assured by their subjection to the ruling ideology)

(NB Marx had a very high regard for Aristotle)

(religious, ethical, etc.)

(ideology = an imaginary relation to real relations)

(for everyone, i.e. for all those who live in an ideological representation of ideology, which reduces ideology to ideas endowed by definition with a spiritual existence)

(*dispositif*)

(a subject endowed with a consciousness in which he freely forms or freely recognizes ideas in which he believes)

(material)

(once it was material in the ordinary sense of the term)

("no one is willingly evil")

(however perverse)

(for woe to him who brings scandal into the world!)

(such and such an individual)

(consciousness)

(except in the sense in which one might say a government or a glass is overturned)

(of a non-ministerial type)

(insofar as they are endowed with an ideal or spiritual existence)

(set out in the order of its real determination)

(the subject)

(which may function under other names: e.g., as the soul in Plato, as God, etc.)

(regional or class)

(*which defines it*)

(a tautological proposition)

(for all scientific discourse is by definition a subject-less discourse, there is no "Subject of science" except in an ideology of science)

(obviousnesses are always primary)

(free, ethical, etc. ...)

(therefore including the obviousness of the "transparency" of language)

(without appearing to do so, since these are "obviousnesses")

(aloud or in the "still, small voice of conscience")

(its inverse being the function of *misrecognition – méconnaissance*)

(since "it's obvious")

(previous)

((*re*)-*connaissance*)

(and have recognized that he has recognized us)

(a material ritual practice of ideological recognition in everyday life – in France, at least; elsewhere, there are other rituals)

(naturally)

(the hand-shake, the fact of calling you by your name, the fact of knowing, even if I do not know what it is, that you "have" a name of your own, which means that you are recognized as a unique subject, etc.)

(eternal)

(scientific)

(i.e., subject-less)

(it recruits them all)

(it transforms them all)

(or other)

(and not someone else)

(usually behind them)

(nine times out of ten it is the right one)

(to be precise, in the street)

(a quite exceptional case)

(the general case)

(unless one is really a Spinozist or a Marxist, which, in this matter, is to be exactly the same thing)

(for itself)

(for science and reality)

(paternal/maternal conjugal/fraternal)

(presupposing that any meaning can be assigned to that term)

(boy or girl)

(every individual is called by his name, in the passive sense, it is never he who provides his own name)

(Scripture having collected the Word of God, Tradition having transmitted it, Papal Infallibility fixing it for ever on "nice" points)

(to the extent that Pascal's Christ says: "It is for you that I have shed this drop of my blood!")

(eternal life or damnation)

(in the practices of the well-known rituals of baptism, confirmation, communion, confession and extreme unction, etc. ...)

(Yahweh)

(really)

("I am that I am")

(when the subjects wallow in debauchery, i.e. sin)

(the long complaint of the Garden of Olives which ends in the Crucifixion)

(see St. Thomas)

(present and future)

(the Holy Family: the Family is in essence Holy)

(Repressive)

(good)

(whose concrete forms are realized in the Ideological State Apparatuses)

(*das Bestehende*)

(1)

(2)

(*free*)

(*freely*)

("naturally": outside the prayer, i.e. outside the ideological intervention)

(*méconnue*)

(ideology = misrecognition/ignorance)

(above all the effect of legal-ethical ideology)

(= class)

(as "poor" as those which, according to Marx, define production *in general*, or in Freud, define *the* unconscious *in general*)

Herbert Marcuse
An Essay on Liberation

(though not of revolution)
(this essay will stress the obstacles and "delays")
(*la contestation permanente*)

(and this time a spectre
which haunts not only the bourgeoisie
but all exploitative bureaucracies)

(and particularly Marxian theory)
(if any)
(the workers)

(itself a dimension
of the infrastructure of society)
(voluntary inasmuch as it is introjected

into the individuals)
(the potential of liberation)
(and thereby concepts)

(and of their validation)
(for all
practical purposes)

(though with considerable ambivalence)
(steered but not abolished
by government intervention)

(the International is the late concretization
of the abstract
philosophical concept

of 'man as man,' human being,
'*Gattungswesen*', which plays such a decisive role
in Marx's and Engel's early writings)

(and not only the organized)
(though not as
the builder)

(freedom)
(*soviets*)
(sublimation)

(and the aesthetic truth)
(artistic)
(ontological)

(*Vollkommenheit*)
(*Spiegelung*)
(*Lebensteigernd*)

(space and time)
(and beyond the power)
(material)

(in a literal sense!)
(cooking!)
(productive in their receptivity)

(language in the wider sense
which includes words,
gestures, images, tones)

(if not denial)
(used and abused)
(in its essence

lily-white ever since Plato)
(in which Kant
saw the token of freedom)

(by virtue of which
art has the power
of reconciliation with the *status quo*)

(which militated against the realization
of the truth, of the cognitive
force of art)

(I shall use 'art' throughout
as including the visual arts as well as
literature and music)

(*schöner Schein*)
(*Besitzvorststellungen*)
(*die Dinglichkeiten*)

(in spite of the fact
that so much of art
is obviously not beautiful!)

(it may even deter
the unsublimated drive!)
(matter)

(sense)
(though it may be invisible)
(and of the 'nature' of man)

(as they do
after a brief *katharsis*,
in the psyche)

(as in every stage
of the development
of freedom did)

(and its avant-gardist
white development)
(which, to a considerable extent,

was also operative in the great
illusionist art)
(that is to say,

a subverting force)
(the artistic, modernistic banks,
office buildings, kitchens, salesrooms, and salespeople, etc.)

(and hated)
(often disorganized)
(or rather contraction)

(from the organized industrial
working classes to militant minorities)
(probably intermittent and preliminary)

(relatively)
(note the smooth fusion
of love, kill, research, and saleable)

(and the unconscious)
(even of its culture
and ideology)

(and the unconscious)
(and the rise of a Negro bourgeoisie)
(in terms of the capitalist system)

(*Confédération Générale du Travail*)
(and apparently increasing)
(in Spain, in Latin American countries)

(a minority
of the students everywhere)
(and passing!)

(urgent enough
by themselves;
we shall come back to them subsequently)

(as it was so often
in the past)
(towards the object world,

towards reality)
('bourgeois' democracy, representative
government)

(however limited in practice)
(perhaps even defend)
(and even a little beyond it)

(without altogether neglecting or even minimizing
the more material
and economic aspects)

(or type of nation-state)
(enforceable)
(according to the *Los Angeles Times*,

25 June, 1968)
(weakest and most diffused
of all historical oppositions)

(no matter how
'benevolent')
(presumably they should have stayed in)

(presumably Americans only attack
in broad daylight, don't disturb
the sleep of the enemies

and don't kill Vietnamese boys)
(in Indonesia)
(as *Untermensch*)

(the domino theory!)
(anonymous)
(and command)

(like the ideas of liberty,
equality, fraternity advanced
by the revolutionary bourgeoisie)

(sustained high productivity; large
markets; neo-colonialism; administered democracy)
(relatively)

(which is part of the required
sanity)
(quite apart from their ideational validity)

(abolition of private ownership
and control of the means
of production: planned economy)

(which is an important aspect
of the general containment policy
pursued by the established societies)

(or to introduce)
(and perhaps not at all)
(and socialist?)

(this level could be considerably lower   ·
than that of advanced capitalist productivity,
which is geared to obscene affluence and waste)

(time)
(and only in terms of the latter)
(more or less effectively)

OIL FOR FOOD

"I called you 'fellow investor' just now for a reason."

The idea of north just shifted north.

Who took it, and how are you going to get it back?

"There was a redundancy of exploiters."

I'm writing this letter to explain my failure to act like a human being.

Water for power.

"It was much more my style to find sand in my eyes."

Steel, unlike coffee and chocolate.

A pension plan sinking like a ship's anchor offshored to Foxconn's supply chain.

"Expansive austerity."

Toxic assets for a toxic personality end-of-decade bonus!

"The shoes speak for themselves and need no further explanation."

Stuck in the rust-belt blues again.

"Architecture as a slap in the face to reinforced concrete."

Now it is Yemen.

Controversy public square with a barbeque with the president – all non-contract workers welcome!

Your building speaks Spanish, it learned it while it was being built.

[G.W. Bush quotation deleted here]

Albania 59.3%, Angola 16.2%, Argentina 43.6%.

"It's their country after all," even if we hollowed it out like a skull.

To counter the land claim, they claimed golf as their cultural heritage.

The first country I watched get invaded on camera was Grenada.

"What was done to my country was very un-American": an American.

"Nixon" as verb.

Fully clothed selfie.

"A fresh coat of paint can garner a return on investment up to 300%."

If you think you know what debt is, you don't know what love is (mountain high).

How deep is the city?

"It was completely renovated inside and it was modern, which is something buyers are really looking for today."

All Yesterday's Oligarchies are tinpot generals with psychopathic special forces and a driver – today, dig the new breed!

If the customers can see you, it is invasion of privacy.

We, we can be owners, but not for just one day.

"I wanted to create a room where just sitting there feels like you're doing something."

Hey Mr. Pipeline, plug a leak for me in your environmentally friendly way!

"I was given the classic geographer's tour of the city."

Bahrain 54.3%, Bolivia 34.6%, Bulgaria 16.2%.

Down south, the workers collectivize the factory, up north the middle classes unite?

"Events are always – original, but they get reabsorbed ..."

Is that Bill Gates on the world music guitar?

Great moments in the history of pop music from rainy cities, volume one.

"Property is eternal, like every negation ..."

Force, of course, or other economic means.

"Fear" sticks to those bodies, borders.

"This process annihilates light manufacturing
activity" and time.

Ask the architects what is minimal.

"The Spruce Street tower may be a block of flats for the
well-off, but it brings an energy to the skyline from which
the whole of New York benefits."

When Classic Rockification hits post-Fordism, you get a
different Detroit.

"In fact, we could chart our major life events by
acquisitions ..."

A table does not make itself (nor can it handle complex
supply chains and marketing).

Soon we will be ship breaking, that is a lyricism
we are living.

"When you think of class warfare, you probably think of
inciting anger, resentment and jealousy among the have-
nots against the haves."

I enter an Iceland period.

"Unhappy workers."

Canada 84.6%, Chile 11.9%, China 31.7%.

I loved your novel, it's you I can't stand (and that's where the marketing campaign stops).

Trickle-down architecture.

"Is it really necessary to say something about the individual here?"

Daniel Ortega and the return of Daniel Ortega.

Yes, flesh over a titanium skeletal device, since you asked.

"Cual es tu huelga?"

Captain, dear captain, were you asleep at the wheel or drunk at the rudder?

"This administration stands for more than finding another country to go to war against."

Good morning, Syria.

(Not even "with.")

Mark Carney and the triumphalism of Mark Carney.

"Any space that is organized around the monument is colonized and oppressed."

And who remembers Maurice Bishop?

Slovakia, naturally (alone again).

Zurich in Vancouver, reserves in the townships, pockets
of poverty, haunted penthouses gaze at rusted hulks and
westward owners sob at the wonders of nature.

From refugee to criminal in one step (the waterfront).

"The ranch has an organic, love-the-planet, old hippie vibe –
at least once you get past the guardhouse."

Book clubs.

I have not reached the point in my life where I can, in terms
of libidinal economy, enjoy Bananarama.

It was a cruel cruel summer in 1983 when the "new reality"
of restraint was top of the biopolitical pops.

Ecuador 20.9%, Egypt 88%, Estonia 5.7%.

The city centre, slowly moving east, as if nature wanted the
working-class off the waterfront.

All the parenthetical remarks want their cultural
heritage back.

As the dead prey upon us they still find time for a rigorous
workout regime!

Call me impaled, Ishmael.

The Austrian television premiere of Adam Sandler's
Little Nicky is a sad sad cultural imperialism.

But we are all above blame, south of liberalism, north of
spatializing an idea.

"With the birth of the market in loft living ..."

Things and the return of things – beautiful documented
supply chain!

My father's Timex.

Little Willie John ends dead in Seattle.

Pack up your labour-power in a "sturdy waxed American
cotton" worker's bag ($378.00).

"They burnt some flags, but for us, burning flags is not a
security issue, it's an environmental issue."

At two dollars a day, a European cow earns more than a
billion people.

Consumer transparency, activist investors, primitive
accumulation in the kitchen, "which encourages good
practice among corporates and NGOs alike."

Martha Stewart and the return of Martha Stewart.

"Peppered" is just another verb for "shot" – as a noun it's another thing with a history.

Nature leans in, it wants its hammer back.

Mexico has now made the world's richest man ("good practice").

"He currently works with PlaceSpeak, an online location-based community consultation platform."

Finland 53%, Germany 81.9%, Greece 156.9%.

Total urbanization! says the World Health Organization.

"The workers themselves spent most of the morning erecting a protective plywood barrier around the building's perimeter."

"Deliriously flavourful mouthfuls of Thai Baked Lentils with Paneer, Spinach, Coconut and Polenta."

Pleasure, it fails us now (but I see it is working pretty good for you)!

Stop the tyranny of serial pleasure!

Banalization is not possible!

Brazil wakes up to another modernism, this time on the streets.

Nicaragua returns without a hat, but with the same moustache (*sin sombrero, con bigote*).

At the tipping point of neoliberalism (I recklessly write this on April 1, 2007, and you may read it any time in the future), a new science: happiness economics.

And today, the *New York Times* asks us, "Can Poor People Be Taught to Save?"

Can you ask your computer if it is an anti-Estonian cyber spy?

When was Detroit?

Up north, we look to the south, horizontally.

We don't want your ideas, just your labour, temporarily.

What do you mean, white man?

India 49.6%, Japan 214%, Libya 3.5%.

I guess Supertramp was right all along.

"There is a worse and better police."

So many livers of poets, of Marxists, crash against the market – I keep mine close to my heart.

"I am not building condominiums, I am building three sculptures for people to live in."

The market prefers bodies without organs.

The city quickly solves its yacht-docking shortage!

Decent.

Robert Mugabe and the return of Mugabe.

Hegemony is hard, it's a hard job but someone's
got to benefit.

"Pages 2 to 9 have been hidden by the current
document owner."

I was born for loving you, land art, Group B rally, and post-
conceptual practices.

"Collectivize" as poetic language and a syntactic trick that
needs cruelty-free flesh.

My dad's adze, through a cedary haze, takes me back to the
days of shakes and planks.

Thus I remake the seventies in my own image, recuperating
a sense of self as if I had written my name on all
of his tools.

My file.

"This is my truth, based on what I believed back then and
which I only saw more clearly today."

Johnny Nash as *operaismo* soul, leaving the factory gates with a wayward dog entering from the left.

I Maximus to the mortgage brokers.

I Oppen to the party operatives.

I Lowther to the overlords!

Mexico 35.9%, Norway 29.7%, Poland 123.6%.

Haters gonna hate, potato eaters gonna peel, and itinerate farm workers gonna be tied to short-term visas.

"From our study, there is clearly no silver bullet to impede gentrification ..."

Hey, regional ingredients!

Somebody loan me a dime, I've got to call my old used-to-be to check on our GDP-to-debt ratio.

The proud marching language of a nation, flanked and chipped like a boatload of border guards hunkered in the harbour, under watch.

Happenings, seventies body art, and soft architecture, please annihilate micro-lofts in the name of the future (which you never made it to).

Mike Tyson and the return of Mike Tyson.

I live in a creative city, sir, and I serve the creative class.

"For a coin, the road from the mint is also the path to the melting pot."

Book learning: Has it been historically undervalued? We want your opinion!

More than a feeling!

The utterance is always half Mark Zuckerberg's.

Now it is Yemen again.

I am an independent contractor with ownership of my own power washer.

We don't want your "totalizing moment" (teachable moment), we don't want your street control.

We educated ourselves, like wolves, like one and several wolves, like a pack of effing wolves around terrycloth tables in the bar ringing the great harbour!

"This article is not nearly as informative as it first appeared."

It is an empire on its own, this loser's game, this military complex in one country, so please do not darken my door.

The city wakes up, and people follow filled with horizontal love.

Stagflation, let's not let that happen to you and me, even before the end of capitalism as we know it.

Qatar 32.8%, Russia 7.7%, Spain 84.1%.

Get your Maserati outta my pastrami, get your Porsche outta my borscht, get your Tesla outta my slaw, etc.

"Art galleries moving into a low-income area is often ..."

The police, in so many voices.

Drunken LinkedIn rampage.

Andy Warhol and the return of Warhol.

"There is no room here for disappointment."

Berlusconi and the return of Berlusconi and the return of Berlusconi.

Cheney's artificial valve rejects heart.

"For centuries, business leaders have been inept when writers, intellectuals and politicians attacked capitalism ..."

I'd love to blame you, you are so blamable, so utterly flammable.

"The Programme had been required to meet 'an almost impossible series of challenges,' using some $46 billion of Iraqi export earnings on behalf of the Iraqi people."

Are you now, or have you ever, worked for $7.50 an hour?

"Former U.S. secretary of state Henry Kissinger will present the award to Mr. Harper."

Turkey 36.1%, United States 72.5%, Venezuela 26.8%.

We're looking at a crisis bigger than Tuesday.

"It could just as credibly be said that 'the world owes this money to itself,' and so owes nothing."

As the sun dips in the west, I salute you all – readers, wrenchers, makers, reproducers, wolves – with a love that is fracked gas blue.

"Fuller fullness."

ACKNOWLEDGEMENTS

Grateful acknowledgement is made to the editors and
publishers of various publications in which some of the
material in this book first appeared: *Armed Cell* 3, edited by
Brian Ang; *M'aidez*, Press Release Collective, May 2012; *Open
Letter* ser. 14, no. 8 (Spring 2012), "Negotiating the Social
Bond of Poetics," edited by Nancy Gillespie and Peter Jaeger;
OPEN TEXT: Canadian Poetry in the 21st Century, edited by
Roger Farr; *West Coast Line* 57 (2008), edited by Fred Wah;
West Coast Line 51 (2006), "Poetry and the Long Neoliberal
Moment"; *The Capilano Review* 3, no. 18 (Fall 2012), edited
by Brook Houglum.

A section of "The Vestiges" was printed as a broadside, designed
by The Emergency Response Unit, for Scream in High Park,
Toronto, 2010. Thanks, too, to Barry McKinnon, who made a
broadside for our joint reading at the College of New Caledonia
in Prince George on 26 March 2010.

No book is the product of a single moment or event and this
book is itself saturated with the conversations and labour of
others: Brian Ang, Michael Barnholden, Sabine Bitter, Christian
Bök, Clint Burnham, David Buuk, Louis Cabri, Steve Collis,
Kevin Davies, Roger Farr, Robert Fitterman, Gregory Gibson,
Jamie Hilder, Alfredo Jaar, Nils Jensen, Smaro Kamboureli,
Cindi Katz, Dorothy Trujillo Lusk, Belen Martin Lucas, Michèle
Mouton, Cecily Nicholson, Mark Nowak, Christian Parenti,
Stefan Römer, Jordan Scott, Lytle Shaw, Kathy Slade, Neil Smith,
Rodrigo Toscano, Urban Subjects, Helmut Weber, and Van.Act!
(for their "Right to the City: Cops, Condos, Gentrification &
the Alternatives" gathering). And, of course, others ...

A NOTE ON THE POEMS

The Vestiges

This book is an investigation into poetic research and social expression in precarious times. Feeling that we were living through great social changes from 2001 to 2013 whose implications where somehow simultaneously underestimated or overdramatized, I found myself reading late-modernist poems that took a more embedded perspective on society and its shifts. The position of the poets in these works presumed a sort of clarity *despite* the complexity of their present. I wondered what it would be like to do a *remake* of this type of poem. Or, in other less poetic words, I wanted to write in a poetic form from a Fordist time in precarious and post-Fordist times. What forms of social expression would this remake open to me? How would the writing of the poem position me in relation to the language and images of neoliberalism? What would that long interlocking serial form, with its particular rhythms of accumulation and cresting, and with its author located in the swirl of social processes and grounded in a place that is simultaneously stable yet eroding, tell me (and hopefully other readers) about our own stake in the present? There are echoes of many poems in *The Vestiges*, but consistently it is George Oppen's *Of Being Numerous* that struck me as a poetic form and a social stance that reverberated across our own uneven present.

"I welcome every opinion based on scientific criticism"

This is a text made from "all of the sentences containing the first-person pronoun in Marx's *Capital*, Volume 1, excluding the prefaces, the footnotes, and sentences quoted from other authors, but including the characterizations of the capitalist and the worker)." By isolating the sentences in Marx's book that have a form of first-person expression, what kind of writer emerges? Is there a residual humanist amongst the formulas and the calculations (or, is the "radical" split of Marx's work not so definitive)? I also wanted to test Helmut Draxler's statement that "not every form of art today can be understood as expression, contemplation or direct transfer of energy"[1] through its reversal: could a text (*Capital*, Volume 1) that is not understood as an expressive text actually be worked into one? And could it then be able to speak back to itself and its readers? It turns out, there is a funny, angry, kind of anxious, sort of repetitive, and very clear writer in *Capital*. I was curious, as well, to see if these first-person sentences could stand as a synopsis, or a personalized lecture, of the whole book – I hope they do. Jason Starnes and Cameron Fediuk also went through Volume 1 to find these sentences – it took a surprising amount of labour-time from us.

---

1   Helmut Draxler, "A Culture of Division: Artistic Research as a Problem," in *Faith Is the Place: the Urban Cultures of Global Prayers* (Berlin: MetroZones 11/ b_books, 2012), 124.

The Parenthetical

This text has its genesis in a 2008 exhibition at SFU Gallery,
Burnaby, *Less is More: The Poetics of Erasure*, curated by
Bill Jeffries and Ariana Kelly. I had been reading the small
editions of Herbert Marcuse's work, such as *The Aesthetic
Dimension: Toward a Critique of Marxist Aesthetics*,
partially because of their portability, and I began to notice
the wildness of Marcuse's parenthetical remarks. They
stood out as a text within the text. As I began to read
further, I noticed that some authors have charismatic,
enigmatic, and emphatic parenthetical remarks, while
others simply emphasize points, repeat a point in other
words, or add supplementary information. In the chapter
"The Working Day," a wonderfully angry and ironic Marx
emerges in the parenthetical remarks; in Louis Althusser's
excessive parenthetical remarks in his iconic "Ideological
State Apparatus" essay, a reader is pounded with
repression; and Silvia Federici's mid-seventies texts are
in dialogue with Marx, moving into the area of unwaged
labour and its "cost."

But What of the City Itself?

This research poem emerged out of a tendency I noticed in
urban geography texts, or texts giving a history of a city,
in which cities were referred to as if they themselves had
carried out certain actions at a particular time. My research
broadened from there to try and construct a narrative
or city biography of urban change through this type of
sentence. Jason Starnes and Cameron Fediuk also helped
gather these elusive sentences.

Oil for Food

This text closes out a serial poem that has been spread out over several books – *Dwell*, *Transnational Muscle Cars*, and some chapbooks. So long, I've enjoyed this poetic form as a way of thinking.

A Note on the Design

The Vestiges takes mid-sixties New Directions Paperback poetry books as its design model. I was drawn to their clarity and seriousness. Particular design references are found in Denise Levertov's *O Taste and See* (designed by David Ford), George Oppen's *The Materials* (designed by Gilda Kuhlman), and *Of Being Numerous* (design curiously unattributed). Accordingly, we chose Sabon, a typeface designed in 1966 by Jan Tschichold, to set the interior. The back cover copy is derived from an amalgam of New Directions Paperback Originals. The cover image is a detail from Alfredo Jaar's series *Searching for Gramsci* (2004); the full image is reproduced on the frontispiece. Like much of Jaar's work, it invokes place, politics, and a haunting of what is not visible.

SOURCES

But What of the City Itself?

69 — Marcela López Levy, *We Are Millions: Neo-Liberalism and New Forms of Political Action in Argentina* (London: LAB, 2004), 43.

David Harvey, *Paris, Capital of Modernity* (New York: Routledge, 2006), 3.

Robert Venturi, Denise Scott Brown, and Steven Izenour, *Learning from Las Vegas* (Cambridge, MA: MIT Press, 1972), 18.

Julie-Anne Boudreau, Roger Keil, and Douglas Young, *Changing Toronto: Governing Urban Neoliberalism* (Toronto: University of Toronto Press, 2009), 46.

Susan S. Fainstein, *The Just City* (Ithaca: Cornell University Press, 2010), 111.

Zbigniew Marcin Kowalewski, "Give Us Back Our Factories! Between Resisting Exploitation and the Struggle for Workers' Power in Poland, 1944–1981," in *Ours to Master and to Own: Workers' Control from the Commune to the Present*, ed. Immanuel Ness and Dario Azzellini (Chicago: Haymarket Books, 2011), 195.

H. D., *Tribute to Freud* (New York: New Directions, 1956), 4.

Coalition of Woodwards Squatters and Supporters, "Call for Second Support Demonstration (09/19)," in "Woodsquat," ed. Aaron Vidaver, *West Coast Line* 37, no. 2 (2003): 37.

70 — Lewis Mumford, *The City in History: Its Origins, Its Transformations, and Its Prospects* (New York: Harcourt, Brace and World, 1961), 352.

St. Clair Drake and Horace R. Cayton, *Black Metropolis: A Study of Negro Life in a Northern City* (New York: Harper and Row, 1962), 38.

Samuel J. Southgate, "From Workers' Self-Management to State Bureaucratic Control: Autogestion in Algeria," in *Ours to Master and to Own: Workers' Control from the Commune to the Present*, ed. Immanuel Ness and Dario Azzellini (Chicago: Haymarket Books, 2011), 233.

Lewis Mumford, *The City in History: Its Origins, Its Transformations, and Its Prospects* (New York: Harcourt, Brace and World, 1961), 288.

Lewis Mumford, *The Culture of Cities* (New York: Harcourt Brace, 1938), 156.

Mike Davis, *Planet of Slums* (London: Verso, 2006), 33.

Rosa Luxemburg, *The Mass Strike* (London: Bookmarks, 1986), 24.

Kevin Lynch, *Good City Form* (Cambridge, MA; MIT Press, 1981), 6.

Mike Davis, *Planet of Slums* (London: Verso, 2006), 13.

71 — Denise Leclerc and Pierre Dessureault, *The 60s in Canada* (Ottawa: National Gallery of Canada, 2005), 23.

Jane Jacobs, *Canadian Cities and Sovereignty Association* (Toronto: Canadian Broadcasting Corporation, 1980), 6.

Julia Bryan-Wilson, *Art Workers: Radical Practice in the Vietnam War Era* (Berkeley: University of California Press, 2009), 114.

Stefan Grissemann, "Countdown to Zero: Before the Avant-Garde: Austrian Visionary Film 1951–1955," in *Film Unframed: A History of Austrian Avant-garde Cinema*, ed. Peter Tscherkassky (Vienna: FilmmuseumSynema Publications, 2012), 45.

Michael Barnholden, *Reading the Riot Act: A Brief History of Riots in Vancouver* (Vancouver: Anvil Press, 2005), 72.

Valerie Fraser, *Building the New World: Studies in the Modern Architecture of Latin America, 1930–1960* (London: Verso, 2000), 113–4.

72 — Karl Marx, "The 18th Brumaire of Louis Bonaparte," in *The Portable Karl Marx*, ed. Eugene Kamenka (Harmondsworth, UK: Penguin Books, 1983), 308.

Benjamin Shepard, "Community Gardens, Convivial Space, and the Seeds of a Radical Democratic Counterpublic," *Democracy, States, and the Struggle for Global Justice*, ed. Heather Gautney, Omar Dahbour, Ashley Dawson, and Neil Smith (New York: Routledge, 2009), 280.

Rachel Carson, *Silent Spring* (New York: Fawcett, 1962), 109.

Marco D'Eramo, *The Pig and the Skyscraper: Chicago, a History of Our Future*, trans. Graeme Thomson (London: Verso, 2002), 239.

Neil Leach, "Architecture or Revolution?" in *Architecture and Revolution: Contemporary Perspectives on Central and Eastern Europe* (New York: Routledge, 1999), 118.

Susan S. Fainstein, *The Just City* (Ithaca: Cornell University Press, 2010), 90.

Susan S. Fainstein, *The Just City* (Ithaca: Cornell University Press, 2010), 150n8.

Renata Salecl, "The State as Work of Art: The Trauma of Ceausecu's Disneyland," in *Architecture and Revolution: Contemporary Perspectives on Central and Eastern Europe*, ed. Neil Leach (New York: Routledge, 1999), 100.

73 — Reyner Banham, *The Architecture of the Well-Tempered Environment* (Chicago: University of Chicago Press, 1969), 184.

Geronimo, *Fire and Flames: A History of the German Autonomist Movement*, trans. Gabriel Kuhn (Oakland: PM Press, 2012), 44.

Geronimo, *Fire and Flames: A History of the German Autonomist Movement*, trans. Gabriel Kuhn (Oakland: PM Press, 2012), 53.

Lewis Mumford, *The City in History: Its Origins, Its Transformations, and Its Prospects* (New York: Harcourt, Brace and World, 1961), 459.

Stephen Graham, *Cities, War, and Terrorism: Towards an Urban Geopolitics* (Malden, MA: Blackwell Publishing, 2004), 59.

Carl E. Schorske, *Fin-de-siècle Vienna: Politics and Culture* (New York: Knopf, 1979), 5–6.

Lewis Mumford, *The City in History: Its Origins, Its Transformations, and Its Prospects* (New York: Harcourt, Brace and World, 1961), 163–4.

Mike Davis, *Planet of Slums* (London: Verso, 2006), 18.

74 — Denise Leclerc and Pierre Dessureault, *The 60s in Canada* (Ottawa: National Gallery of Canada, 2005), 108.

Don Mitchell, *The Right to the City: Social Justice and the Fight for Public Space* (New York: Guilford Press, 2003), 63.

Fulong Wu, Jiang Xu, and Anthony G.O. Yeh, *Urban Development in Post-Reform China: State, Market, and Space* (London: Routledge, 2008), 258.

Patrick Cuninghame, "'Hot Autumn': Italy's Factory Councils and Autonomous Workers' Assemblies, 1970s," in *Ours to Master and to Own: Workers' Control from the Commune to the Present*, ed. Immanuel Ness and Dario Azzellini (Chicago: Haymarket Books, 2011), 332.

Don Mitchell, *The Right to the City: Social Justice and the Fight for Public Space* (New York: Guilford Press, 2003), 168.

Mike Davis, *Planet of Slums* (London: Verso, 2006), 36.

Mike Kurlansky, *Salt: A World History* (New York: Walker and Co., 2002), 116.

Marco D'Eramo, *The Pig and the Skyscraper: Chicago, a History of Our Future*, trans. Graeme Thomson (London: Verso, 2002), 187.

75 — Kristin Ross, *The Emergence of Social Space: Rimbaud and the Paris Commune* (Minneapolis: University of Minnesota Press, 1988), 5.

Mike Davis, *Planet of Slums* (London: Verso, 2006), 14.

Geronimo, *Fire and Flames: A History of the German Autonomist Movement*, trans. Gabriel Kuhn (Oakland: PM Press, 2012), 54.

Stephen Graham, *Cities, War, and Terrorism: Towards an Urban Geopolitics* (Malden, MA: Blackwell Publishing, 2004), 237.

John R. Logan, *Urban China in Transition* (Malden, MA: Blackwell Publishing, 2008), 156.

Bryan D. Palmer, *Canada's 1960s: The Ironies of Identity in a Rebellious Era* (Toronto: University of Toronto, 2009), 197.

Geronimo, *Fire and Flames: A History of the German Autonomist Movement*, trans. Gabriel Kuhn (Oakland: PM Press, 2012), 26.

Valerie Fraser, *Building the New World: Studies in the Modern Architecture of Latin America, 1930–1960* (London: Verso, 2000), 254–5.

76 — Catherine Cooke, "Sources of a Radical Mission in the Early Soviet Profession: Alexei Gan and the Moscow Anarchists," in *Architecture and Revolution: Contemporary Perspectives on Central and Eastern Europe*, ed. Neil Leach (New York: Routledge, 1999), 26.

Mike Davis, *Planet of Slums* (London: Verso, 2006), 54.

Erik Swyngedouw, *Designing the Post-Political City and the Insurgent Polis*, Civic City Cahier 5 (London: Bedford, 2011), 6.

Manfredo Tafuri, *Architecture and Utopia: Design and Capitalist Development*, trans. Barbara Luigia La Penta (Cambridge, MA: MIT Press, 1976), 117.

Manfredo Tafuri, *Architecture and Utopia: Design and Capitalist Development*, trans. Barbara Luigia La Penta (Cambridge, MA: MIT Press, 1976), 116.

Mike Davis, *Planet of Slums* (London: Verso, 2006), 81.

Lewis Mumford, *The Culture of Cities* (New York: Harcourt Brace, 1938), 119.

Ralph Ray Krueger and R. Charles Bryfogle, *Urban Problems: A Canadian Reader* (Toronto: Holt, Rinehart and Winston of Canada, 1971), 340.

77 — Murray Bookchin, *Urbanization Without Cities: The Rise and Decline of Citizenship* (Montreal: Black Rose Books, 1992), 167.

Manuel Castells, *The Urban Question: A Marxist Approach*. Cambridge, MA: MIT Press, 1977), 159.

Mike Davis, *City of Quartz: Excavating the Future in Los Angeles* (London: Verso, 1990), 199.

Manuel Castells, *The Urban Question: A Marxist Approach* (Cambridge, MA: MIT Press, 1977), 109.

Reyner Banham, *The Architecture of the Well-Tempered Environment*. (Chicago: University of Chicago Press, 1969), 141.

Eric Zoran, "The Third Way: The Experiment of Workers' Self-Management in Socialist Yugoslavia," in *Autogestion, or Henri Lefebvre in New Belgrade*, ed. Urban Subjects (Vancouver: Fillip Editions/Sternberg, 2009), 147.

Friedrich Engels, *The Condition of the Working Class in England* (New York: Penguin, 1987), 166.

78 — Sharon Zukin, *Loft Living: Culture and Capital in Urban Change* (New Brunswick, NJ: Rutgers University Press, 1989), 24.

Bill Jeffries, "The Shock of the Old – The Street Photography in Vancouver," in *Unfinished Business: Photographing Vancouver Streets 1955–1985*, ed. Bill Jeffries, Glen Lowry, and Jerry Zaslove (Vancouver: West Coast Line / Presentation House, 2005), 24.

Bryan D. Palmer, *Canada's 1960s: The Ironies of Identity in a Rebellious Era*, (Toronto: University of Toronto Press, 2009), 402.

Andrew Ross, *Bird on Fire: Lessons from the World's Least Sustainable City* (Oxford: Oxford University Press, 2011), 81.

Carl E. Schorske, *Fin-de-siècle Vienna: Politics and Culture* (New York: Knopf, 1979), 79.

Peter Robinson, "Workers Councils in Portugal, 1974–1975," in *Ours to Master and to Own: Workers' Control from the Commune to the Present*, ed. Immanuel Ness and Dario Azzellini (Chicago: Haymarket Books, 2011), 264.

Marco D'Eramo, *The Pig and the Skyscraper: Chicago, a History of Our Future*, trans. Graeme Thomson (London: Verso, 2002), 180.

Reyner Banham, *Los Angeles; the Architecture of Four Ecologies* (New York: Harper and Row, 1971), 16–17

79 — John R. Logan, *Urban China in Transition* (Malden, MA: Blackwell Publishing, 2008), 142.

Susan S. Fainstein, *The Just City* (Ithaca: Cornell University Press, 2010), 115.

Murray Bookchin, *Urbanization Without Cities: The Rise and Decline of Citizenship* (Montréal: Black Rose Books, 1992), 160.

Geronimo, *Fire and Flames: A History of the German Autonomist Movement*, trans. Gabriel Kuhn (Oakland: PM Press, 2012), 154.

Neil Smith, "Preface," in *Autogestion, or Henri Lefebvre in New Belgrade* (Vancouver: Fillip Editions/Sternberg, 2009), 86.

Catherine Cooke, "Sources of a Radical Mission in the Early Soviet Profession: Alexei Gan and the Moscow Anarchists," in *Architecture and Revolution: Contemporary Perspectives on Central and Eastern Europe*, ed. Neil Leach (New York: Routledge, 1999), 18.

Stevphen Shukaitis, David Graeber, and Erika Biddle, *Constituent Imagination: Militant Investigations//Collective Theorization* (Oakland, CA: AK Press, 2007), 167.

80 — Marco D'Eramo, *The Pig and the Skyscraper: Chicago, a History of Our Future*, trans. Graeme Thomson (London: Verso, 2002), 289.

Arjun Appadurai, *Fear of Small Numbers: An Essay on the Geography of Anger* (Durham: Duke University Press, 2006), 96.

Nato Thompson, Jeffrey Kastner, and Trevor Paglen, *Experimental Geography*. (Brooklyn: Melville House, 2008), 83.

Mike Davis, *Dead Cities, and Other Tales* (New York: New Press, 2002), 407.

Geronimo, *Fire and Flames: A History of the German Autonomist Movement*, trans. Gabriel Kuhn (Oakland: PM Press, 2012), 55.

David Harvey, *A Brief History of Neoliberalism* (Oxford: Oxford University Press, 2005), 57.

Elaine Bernard, "Recipe for Anarchy: British Columbia's Telephone Workers' Occupation of 1981," in *Ours to Master and to Own: Workers' Control from*